365 Best
Inspirational Quotes

Daily Motivation for Your Best Year Ever

New York Times Bestselling Author
K. E. Kruse

www.KevinKruse.com

Wholehearted Leadership Press

PHILADELPHIA

365 Best Inspirational Quotes. —2nd ed.

Your Free Gift
ONLINE VIDEO TRAINING
*"6 Things Successful People Do
To Get & Stay Motivated"*

As a way of saying *thanks* for buying this book, I'm offering free online training exclusive to my readers.

I've personally recorded a 20-minute video that reveals
*"6 Things Successful People Do
To Get & Stay Motivated"*.

Just go to this link to watch the video:
www.KevinKruse.com\bonusquotes

—KEVIN KRUSE
New York Times Bestselling Author

CONTENTS

YOUR DAILY DOSE OF INSPIRATION

Would you like a daily "vitamin" that inspires you and motivates you to greatness?

I can remember clearly how scared I was the first day I started my business when nothing was certain. I was alone and literally started my company with just a phone, a cheap laptop, a credit card and a copy of Tony Robbins' *Unlimited Power* on my desk.

Whenever I needed a dose of motivation—which was frequent in the early days—I would randomly open to a page in Tony Robbins' book and read a sentence or two. Five years later I sold that business for almost two million dollars. And to this day I remember those Robbins' quotes.

Later, I decided to fulfill my dream of being an author. Staring at a blank page is hard. Pushing through frequent writer's block is harder. I would once again read quotes on creativity and perseverance from famous authors to push my way through. I was fortunate and eventually my book on leadership became a *New York Times* bestseller.

Today, quotes help motivate me to live healthy, to be an effective leader, to be mindful and to always have an "attitude of gratitude."

I wish I could guarantee that this book will make you rich, skinny and happy. But you know I can't do that.

All I can offer is the condensed wisdom of some of history's greatest, most successful people. I still turn to their advice for encouragement myself. Whether or not you'll take the inspiration from these words and turn it into action…well, that will be up to you.

- Kevin Kruse
  New York Times Bestselling Author

Bucks County, PA, USA

BEST 365 QUOTATIONS

Your time is limited,
so don't waste it
living someone else's life.
–Steve Jobs

2
I believe that the only courage anybody ever
needs is the courage to follow your own dreams.
–Oprah Winfrey

3
I've missed more than 9000 shots in my career.
I've lost almost 300 games. 26 times I've been
trusted to take the game winning shot and
missed. I've failed over and over and over again
in my life. And that is why I succeed.
–Michael Jordan

4
Yesterday is history. Tomorrow is a mystery.
Today is a gift.
That's why it's called the present.
–Unknown

5
Don't wait. The time will never be just right.
–Napoleon Hill

6

*Life isn't about getting
and having,
it's about giving and being.*
–Kevin Kruse

7
If you can dream it, you can achieve it.
–Zig Ziglar

8
How am I going to live today in order to create
the tomorrow I'm committed to?
–Anthony Robbins

9
Too many of us are not living our dreams
because we are living our fears.
–Les Brown

10
Build your own dreams,
or someone else will hire you to build theirs.
–Farrah Gray

11

*I've learned that people will
forget what you said,
people will forget what you did,
but people will never forget how
you made them feel.*
–Maya Angelou

12
Life is 10% what happens to me
and 90% of how I react to it.
–Charles Swindoll

13
Go confidently in the direction of your dreams.
Live the life you have imagined.
–Henry David Thoreau

14
Life is what happens to you
while you're busy making other plans.
–John Lennon

15
The best time to plant a tree was 20 years ago.
The second best time is now.
–Chinese Proverb

16
Whatever the mind of man can conceive
and believe, it can achieve.
–Napoleon Hill

17
Dream big and dare to fail.
–Norman Vaughan

18
If you want to lift yourself up,
lift up someone else.
–Booker T. Washington

19
A good plan violently executed now is better
than a perfect plan executed next week.
–George Patton

20

*Two roads diverged in a wood,
and I–I took the one less traveled
by, And that has made
all the difference.*
–Robert Frost

21
A journey of a thousand miles must begin
with a single step.
–Lao Tzu

22
What would you do if you weren't afraid?
–Spencer Johnson

23
Become the kind of leader that people
would follow voluntarily;
even if you had no title or position.
–Brian Tracy

24
A goal without a plan is just a wish.
–Larry Elder

25

Twenty years from now you will be more disappointed by the things that you didn't do than by the ones you did do, so throw off the bowlines, sail away from safe harbor, catch the trade winds in your sails. Explore, Dream, Discover.
–Mark Twain

26
A leader is best when people barely know he exists, when his work is done, his aim fulfilled, they will say: we did it ourselves.
–Lao Tzu

27
A man who dares to waste one hour of life has not discovered the value of life.
–Charles Darwin

28
A person who never made a mistake never tried anything new.
–Albert Einstein

29
A truly rich man is one whose children run into his arms when his hands are empty.
–Unknown

30
A true leader has the confidence to stand alone,
the courage to make tough decisions, and the
compassion to listen to the needs of others.
–Douglas MacArthur

31
All the forces in the world are not so powerful
as an idea whose time has come.
–Victor Hugo

32
Anyone can hold the helm when the sea is calm.
–Publilius Syrus

33
A goal is not always meant to be reached;
it often serves simply as something to aim at.
–Bruce Lee

34
Definiteness of purpose
is the starting point of all achievement.
–W. Clement Stone

35
Fall seven times and stand up eight.
–Japanese Proverb

36
If one advances confidently in the direction of
his dreams, and endeavors to live the life he has
imagined, he will meet with a
success unexpected in common hours.
–Henry Thoreau

37
Goals are dreams with deadlines.
–Diana Scharf Hunt

38
I am not a product of my circumstances.
I am a product of my decisions.
–Stephen Covey

39
I cannot give you the formula for success, but I
can give you the formula for failure, which is:
Try to please everybody.
–Herbert Swope

40
I recommend to you to take care of the minutes;
for hours will take care of themselves.
–Lord Chesterfield

41
If you're offered a seat on a rocket ship,
don't ask what seat! Just get on.
–Sheryl Sandberg

42
Impossible is a word to be found
only in the dictionary of fools.
–Napoleon Bonaparte

43
The only way to do great work
is to love what you do.
–Steve Jobs

44
It is better to have lived one day as a tiger
than a thousand years as a sheep.
–Tibetan saying

45
It's not the years in your life that count.
It's the life in your years.
–Abraham Lincoln

46

My interest in life comes from setting myself huge, apparently unachievable challenges and trying to rise above them.
–Richard Branson

47
Lead me, follow me, or get out of my way.
–General George Patton

48
Money is a wonderful thing,
but it is possible to pay too high a price for it.
–Alexander Bloch

49
Never tell people how to do things.
Tell them what to do and they will surprise you
with their ingenuity.
–General George Patton

50
Shoot for the moon. Even if you miss,
you'll land among the stars.
–Les Brown

51

Life is not measured by the number of breaths we take, but by the moments that take our breath away.
–Maya Angelou

52
Not the cry, but the flight of a wild duck,
leads the flock to fly and follow.
–Chinese Proverb

53
Strive not to be a success,
but rather to be of value.
–Albert Einstein

54
Take care of the minutes and the hours
will take care of themselves.
–Lord Chesterfield

55
The greatest dreams are always unrealistic.
–Will Smith

56
The mind is everything.
What you think you become.
–Buddha

57
The question isn't who is going to let me;
it's who is going to stop me.
–Ayn Rand

58
The two most important days in your life
are the day you are born
and the day you find out why.
–Mark Twain

59
There are no traffic jams along the extra mile.
–Roger Staubach

60
There is nothing so useless as doing efficiently
that which should not be done at all.
–Peter Drucker

61
There is only one way to avoid criticism:
do nothing, say nothing, and be nothing.
–Aristotle

62
Time is the coin of your life. It is the only coin
you have, and only you can determine how it
will be spent. Be careful lest you let
other people spend it for you.
–Carl Sandburg

63
We become what we think about.
–Earl Nightingale

64

What's money? A man is a success if he gets up in the morning and goes to bed at night and in between does what he wants to do.
–Bob Dylan

65

Whatever you are, be a good one.
–Abraham Lincoln

66

Whatever you can do, or dream you can, begin it. Boldness has genius, power and magic in it.
–Johann Wolfgang von Goethe

67

Where there is no vision, the people perish.
–Proverbs 29:18

68

When I was 5 years old, my mother always told me that happiness was the key to life. When I went to school, they asked me what I wanted to be when I grew up.- I wrote down 'happy'. They told me I didn't understand the assignment, and I told them they didn't understand life.
–John Lennon

69
Whether you think you can
or you think you can't, you're right.
–Henry Ford

70
You become what you believe.
–Oprah Winfrey

71
You miss 100% of the shots you don't take.
–Wayne Gretzky

72
You will never find time for anything.
If you want time you must make it.
–Charles Buxton

73
Change your thoughts and you
change your world.
–Norman Vincent Peale

74
Never doubt that a small group of thoughtful,
concerned citizens can change world. Indeed it is
the only thing that ever has.
–Margaret Mead

75
Neither success nor failure are ever final.
–Roger Babson

76
You are not defined by your past.
You are prepared by your past.
–Joel Osteen

77
Always do what you are afraid to do.
–Ralph Waldo Emerson

78
We tend to forget that happiness doesn't come
as a result of getting something we don't have,
but rather recognizing and appreciating
what we do have.
–Friedrich Koenig

79
Nobody can go back and start a new beginning,
but anyone can start today and make
a new ending.
–Maria Robinson

80
Seek opportunity, not security.
A boat in a harbor is safe, but in time
its bottom will rot out.
–H. Jackson Brown Jr.

81
Don't worry about failure;
you only have to be right once.
–Drew Houston

82
I must follow the people.
Am I not their leader?
–Benjamin Disraeli

83
If you want to be happy,
set a goal that commands your thoughts,
liberates your energy and inspires your hopes.
–Andrew Carnegie

84
People buy into the leader
before they buy into the vision.
–John Maxwell

85

*Don't ask what the world needs.
Ask what makes you come alive,
and go do it. Because what the
world needs is people who
have come alive.*
–Howard Thurman

86
The art of leadership is saying no,
not saying yes. It is very easy to say yes.
–Tony Blair

87
To command is to serve,
nothing more and nothing less.
–Andre Malraux

88
We are too busy mopping the floor
to turn off the faucet.
–Unknown

89
What you do has far greater impact
than what you say.
–Stephen Covey

90
You manage things; you lead people.
–Rear Admiral Grace Murray Hopper

91
A day wasted on others
is not wasted on one's self.
–Charles Dickens

92
A good leader is a person who takes
a little more than his share of the blame
and a little less than his share of the credit.
–John C. Maxwell

93
A leader is a dealer in hope.
–Napoleon Bonaparte

94
A leader is one who knows the way,
goes the way, and shows the way.
–John C. Maxwell

95
A leader takes people where they want to go.
A great leader takes people where they don't
necessarily want to go, but ought to be.
–Rosalynn Carter

96
A man who wants to lead the orchestra
must turn his back on the crowd.
–Max Lucado

97
All great achievements require time.
–Maya Angelou

98
All successful people have a goal. No one can
get anywhere unless he knows where he wants to
go and what he wants to be or do.
–Norman Vincent Peale

99
All that really belongs to us is time;
even he who has nothing else has that.
–Baltasar Gracián

100
All the flowers of all of the tomorrows
are in the seeds of today.
–Chinese Proverb

101
An unexamined life is not worth living.
–Socrates

102
Arise, awake, stop not until
your goal is achieved.
–Swami Vivekananda

103
An average person with average talents
and ambition and average education, can outstrip
the most brilliant genius in our society, if that
person has clear, focused goals.
–Mary Kay Ash

104
Arriving at one goal
is the starting point to another.
–John Dewey

105
Ask and it will be given to you;
search, and you will find;
knock and the door will be opened for you.
–Jesus

106
Be mindful of how you approach time.
Watching the clock is not the same
as watching the sun rise.
–Sophia Bedford–Pierce

107
Before you are a leader, success is all about
growing yourself. When you become a leader,
success is all about growing others.
–Jack Welch

108
Believe you can and you're halfway there.
–Theodore Roosevelt

109
Certain things catch your eye,
but pursue only those that capture the heart.
–Ancient Indian Proverb

110
Challenges are what make life interesting and
overcoming them is what makes life meaningful.
–Joshua J. Marine

111
Destiny is no matter of chance. It is a matter of
choice. It is not a thing to be waited for;
it is a thing to be achieved.
–William Jennings Bryan

112
Discipline is the bridge between
goals and accomplishment.
–Jim Rohn

113
Do not confuse motion and progress.
A rocking horse keeps moving but does not
make any progress.
–Alfred A. Montapert

114
Do not dwell in the past, do not dream of the
future, concentrate the mind on the
present moment.
–Buddha

115
Do what you can, where you are,
with what you have.
–Teddy Roosevelt

116
Do what you feel in your heart to be right–for
you'll be criticized anyway.
–Eleanor Roosevelt

117
Don't be fooled by the calendar.
There are only as many days in the year as you
make use of. One man gets only a week's value
out of a year while another man gets a
full year's value out of a week.
–Charles Richards

118
Don't be stomping on ants when
you have elephants to feed.
–Peter Turla

119
Don't spend a dollar's worth of time
on a ten-cent decision.
–Peter Turla

120
Dost thou love life? Then do not squander time,
for that's the stuff that life is made of.
–Benjamin Franklin

121
Dreaming, after all, is a form of planning.
–Gloria Steinem

122

*Every child is an artist.
The problem is how to remain an
artist once he grows up.*
–Pablo Picasso

123
Education costs money.
But then so does ignorance.
–Sir Claus Moser

124
Eighty percent of success is showing up.
–Woody Allen

125
Either write something worth reading
or do something worth writing.
–Benjamin Franklin

126
Earn your leadership every day.
–Michael Jordan

127
Either you run the day, or the day runs you.
–Jim Rohn

128
I am endlessly fascinated that playing football
is considered a training ground for leadership,
but raising children isn't.
–Dee Dee Myers

129
Every strike brings me closer
to the next home run.
–Babe Ruth

130
Everything you've ever wanted
is on the other side of fear.
–George Adair

131
Fear melts when you take action
towards a goal you really want.
–Robert Allen

132
Great leaders are not defined by the absence
of weakness, but rather by the presence
of clear strengths.
–John Zenger

133
Half our life is spent trying to find something
to do with the time we have rushed through
life trying to save.
–Will Rogers

134
Happiness is not something readymade.
It comes from your own actions.
–Dalai Lama

135
He who has great power should use it lightly.
–Seneca

136
He who has never learned to obey
cannot be a good commander.
–Aristotle

137
How wonderful it is that nobody need wait
a single moment before starting to
improve the world.
–Anne Frank

138
I am looking for a lot of men
who have an infinite capacity to
not know what can't be done.
–Henry Ford

139
I didn't fail the test.
I just found 100 ways to do it wrong.
–Benjamin Franklin

140
I have learned over the years that when one's
mind is made up, this diminishes fear.
–Rosa Parks

141
I start with the premise that the function of
leadership is to produce more leaders,
not more followers.
–Ralph Nader

142
I would rather die of passion than of boredom.
–Vincent van Gogh

143
The purpose of our lives is to be happy.
–Dalai Lama

144
If one is lucky, a solitary fantasy can totally
transform one million realities.
–Maya Angelou

145
If you aim at nothing, you will hit it every time.
–Zig Ziglar

146
If you do what you've always done,
you'll get what you've always gotten.
–Tony Robbins

147
If you hear a voice within you say "you cannot
paint," then by all means paint and
that voice will be silenced.
–Vincent Van Gogh

148
If you look at what you have in life,
you'll always have more. If you look at what
you don't have in life, you'll never have enough.
–Oprah Winfrey

149
If your actions inspire others to dream more,
learn more, do more and become more,
you are a leader.
–John Quincy Adams

150
In matters of style, swim with the current;
in matters of principle, stand like a rock.
–Thomas Jefferson

151
Live fully. Love openly. Make a difference.
–Brendan Burchard

152
In truth, people can generally make time for
what they choose to do; it is not really the time
but the will that is lacking.
–Sir John Lubbock

153
It doesn't matter where you are coming from.
All that matters is where you are going.
–Brian Tracy

154
It is good to have an end to journey toward;
but it is the journey that matters, in the end.
–Ernest Hemingway

155
It's better to do the right thing slowly
than the wrong thing quickly.
–Peter Turla

156
Know the true value of time; snatch, seize, and
enjoy every moment of it. No idleness, no
laziness, no procrastination; Never put off
till tomorrow what you can do today.
–Lord Chesterfield

157
Know your limits, but never stop
trying to exceed them.
–Unknown

158
Lead and inspire people. Don't try to manage
and manipulate people. Inventories can be
managed but people must be lead.
–Ross Perot

159
Leaders aren't born, they are made.
And they are made just like anything else,
through hard work. And that's the price we'll
have to pay to achieve that goal, or any goal.
–Vince Lombardi

160
Nothing is a waste of time
if you use the experience wisely.
–Rodin

161
Leadership does not always wear
the harness of compromise.
–Woodrow Wilson

162
Nothing is impossible, the word itself says,
"I'm possible!"
–Audrey Hepburn

163
Leadership is the art of getting someone else
to do something you want done
because he wants to do it.
–General Dwight Eisenhower

164
Living without an aim is like
sailing without a compass.
–Alexander Dumas

165
Money, I can only gain or lose. But time I can
only lose. So, I must spend it carefully.
–Unknown

166
Leadership is the capacity
to translate vision into reality.
–Warren Bennis

167

My responsibility is getting all my players playing for the name on the front of the jersey, not the one on the back.
–Unknown

168
Leadership is the key to 99 percent of
all successful efforts.
–Erskine Bowles

169
Life shrinks or expands
in proportion to one's courage.
–Anais Nin

170
Leadership is unlocking people's
potential to become better.
–Bill Bradley

171
Live each day as if it be your last.
–Marcus Aurelius

172
Lost time is never found again.
–Proverb

173
Map out your future, but do it in pencil.
–Jon Bon Jovi

174
Men make history and not the other way around.
In periods where there is no leadership, society
stands still. Progress occurs when courageous,
skillful leaders seize the opportunity to change
things for the better.
–Harry S. Truman

175
Nothing is ours except time.
–Johann Wolfgang von Goethe

176
Obstacles are those frightful things you see
when you take your eyes off your goal.
–Henry Ford

177
Of course I'm ambitious. What's wrong with
that? Otherwise you sleep all day.
–Ringo Starr

178
One of the secrets of life is to make stepping-
stones out of stumbling blocks.
–Jack Penn

179
Our lives begin to end the day we become
silent about things that matter.
–Martin Luther King Jr.

180
Remember that not getting what you want is
sometimes a wonderful stroke of luck.
–Dalai Lama

181
Start where you are. Use what you have.
Do what you can.
–Arthur Ashe

182
The best revenge is massive success.
–Frank Sinatra

183
The distance between insanity and genius is
measured only by success.
–Bruce Feirstein

184
The first responsibility of a leader is to define reality. The last is to say thank you. In between, the leader is a servant.
–Max DePree

185
The key is in not spending time, but in investing it.
–Stephen R. Covey

186
The most common way people give up their power is by thinking they don't have any.
–Alice Walker

187
The person who says it cannot be done should not interrupt the person who is doing it.
–Chinese Proverb

188
The supreme quality of leadership
is integrity.
—Dwight Eisenhower

189
Time is money.
—Benjamin Franklin

190
Time is what we want most,
but what we use worst.
—William Penn

191
Try not. Do or do not. There is no try.
—Yoda

192
Until thought is linked with purpose
there is no intelligent accomplishment.
–James Allen

193
Until we can manage time,
we can manage nothing else.
–Peter Drucker

194
Until you value yourself, you will not value
your time. Until you value your time,
you will not do anything with it.
–M. Scott Peck

195
Vision without action is a daydream.
Action without vision is a nightmare.
–Japanese Proverb

196

There is no such thing as failure.
You either succeed or learn.
–Kevin Kruse

197
We can easily forgive a child who is afraid of
the dark; the real tragedy of life is
when men are afraid of the light.
–Plato

198
We can no more afford to spend major time
on minor things than we can to spend
minor time on major things.
–Jim Rohn

199
When I stand before God at the end of my life,
I would hope that I would not have
a single bit of talent left and could say,
I used everything you gave me.
–Erma Bombeck

200
You can never cross the ocean until you have the
courage to lose sight of the shore.
–Christopher Columbus

201
You can't fall if you don't climb. But there's no joy in living your whole life on the ground.
–Unknown

202
You may be disappointed if you fail, but you are doomed if you don't try.
–Beverly Sills

203
You must get good at one of two things. Planting in the spring or begging in the fall.
–Jim Rohn

204
You take your life in your own hands, and what happens? A terrible thing, no one to blame.
–Erica Jong

205
When I let go of what I am,
I become what I might be.
–Lao Tzu

206
Have the courage to follow your heart
and intuition. They somehow already know
what you truly want to become.
–Steve Jobs

207
The death rate for people who play it safe and
for people who live boldly is the same: 100%.
–Patti Digh

208
There is no passion to be found playing small.
–Nelson Mandela

209
Better three hours too soon,
than one minute too late.
–William Shakespeare

210
You can't use up creativity.
The more you use, the more you have.
–Maya Angelou

211
A cowardly leader is the most dangerous of men.
–Stephen King

212
A deadline is negative inspiration. Still, it's
better than no inspiration at all.
–Rita Mae Brown

213
A good general not only sees the way to victory;
he also knows when victory is impossible.
–Polybius

214
A great leader's courage to fulfill his vision
comes from passion, not position.
–John C. Maxwell

215
A great person attracts great people and knows
how to hold them together.
–Johann Wolfgang Von Goethe

216
As long as I have a want, I have a reason for
living. Satisfaction is death.
–George Bernard Shaw

217
As we look ahead into the next century,
leaders will be those who empower others.
–Bill Gates

218
Between the great things we cannot do and the
small things we will not do,
the danger is that we shall do nothing.
–Adolphe Monod

219
Difficulties increase the nearer
we approach the goal.
–Johann Wolfgang von Goethe

220
Don't say you don't have enough time. You
have exactly the same number of hours per day
that were given to Helen Keller, Pasteur,
Michelangelo, Mother Teresa, Leonardo da
Vinci, Thomas Jefferson, and Albert Einstein.
–H. Jackson Brown

221
Don't be afraid to take a big step if one is
indicated; you can't cross a chasm in
two small jumps.
–David Lloyd George

222
Education is the mother of leadership.
–Wendell Willkie

223
If you want your children to turn out well,
spend twice as much time with them,
and half as much money.
–Abigail Van Buren

224
Effective leadership is not about making
speeches or being liked; leadership is defined by
results not attributes.
–Peter Drucker

225
Effective leadership is putting first things first.
Effective management is discipline,
carrying it out.
–Stephen Covey

226
Even if you're on the right track, you'll get run
over if you just sit there.
–Will Rogers

227
Everything has beauty, but not everyone can see.
–Confucius

228
Few things can help an individual more than to
place responsibility on him, and to let him know
that you trust him.
–Booker T. Washington

229
For time and the world do not stand still.
Change is the law of life. And those who look
only to the past or the present are certain
to miss the future.
–John F. Kennedy

230
Gaining time is gaining everything in love,
trade and war.
–John Shebbeare

231
Goals are not only absolutely necessary to
motivate us. They are essential to really
keep us alive.
–Robert H. Schuller

232
Goals determine what you're going to be.
–Julius Erving

233
He that rises late must trot all day.
–Benjamin Franklin

234
He who gains time gains everything.
–Benjamin Disraeli

235
He who knows most grieves most
for wasted time.
–Dante

236
I am reminded how hollow the label of
leadership sometimes is and how heroic
followership can be.
–Warren Bennis

237
I attribute my success to this: I never gave or took any excuse.
–Florence Nightingale

238
I don't think of the past. The only thing that matters is the everlasting present.
–Somerset Maugham

239
I have been impressed with the urgency of doing. Knowing is not enough; we must apply. Being willing is not enough; we must do.
–Leonardo da Vinci

240
If the wind will not serve, take to the oars.
–Latin Proverb

241
If you don't have time to do it right you must
have time to do it over.
–John Wooden

242
If you don't know where you are going, you will
probably end up somewhere else.
–Lawrence J. Peter

243
If you have built castles in the air, your work
need not be lost; that is where they should be.
Now put the foundations under them.
–Henry David Thoreau

244
In a day, when you don't come across any
problems –you can be sure that you are
travelling in a wrong path.
–Swami Vivekananda

245
It is a mistake to look too far ahead.
Only one link of the chain of destiny can be
handled at a time.
–Winston Churchill

246
It is absurd that a man should rule others,
who cannot rule himself.
–Latin Proverb

247
It is easier to go down a hill than up,
but the view is best from the top.
–Arnold Bennett

248
It is never too late
to be who you might have been.
–George Eliot

249

It is not what you do for your children, but what
you have taught them to do for themselves, that
will make them successful human beings.
–Ann Landers

250

It's not enough to be busy, so are the ants.
The question is, what are we busy about?
–Henry David Thoreau

251

It's your place in the world; it's your life.
Go on and do all you can with it, and make it the
life you want to live.
–Mae Jemison

252

Leadership cannot just go along to get along.
Leadership must meet the moral challenge
of the day.
–Jesse Jackson

253
Leadership is a potent combination of strategy and character. But if you must be without one, be without the strategy.
–Norman Schwarzkopf

254
Life is full of obstacle illusions.
–Grant Frazier

255
Look to the future, because that is where you'll spend the rest of your life.
–George Burns

256
Management is efficiency in climbing the ladder of success; leadership determines whether the ladder is leaning against the right wall.
–Stephen Covey

257
Never leave till tomorrow
that which you can do today.
–Benjamin Franklin

258
Never let yesterday use up today.
–Richard H. Nelson

259
No man will make a great leader who
wants to do it all himself, or to get all
the credit for doing it.
–Andrew Carnegie

260
Nothing else, perhaps, distinguishes effective
executives as much as their tender loving
care of time.
–Peter Drucker

261
Nothing happens until something moves.
–Albert Einstein

262
Once you have mastered time, you will
understand how true it is that most people
overestimate what they can accomplish in a year
–and underestimate what they can achieve
in a decade.
–Anthony Robbins

263
Ordinary people think merely of spending time.
Great people think of using it.
–Unknown

264
People often say that motivation doesn't last.
Well, neither does bathing.
That's why we recommend it daily.
–Zig Ziglar

265
Realize that now, in this moment of time,
you are creating. You are creating your next
moment. That is what's real.
–Sara Paddison

266
Remember no one can make you feel
inferior without your consent.
–Eleanor Roosevelt

267
So much of what we call management consists
in making it difficult for people to work.
–Peter Drucker

268
The battles that count aren't the ones for gold
medals. The struggles within yourself–
the invisible battles inside all of us–
that's where it's at.
–Jesse Owens

269
The future belongs to those who believe in the beauty of their dreams.
–Eleanor Roosevelt

270
The great dividing line between success and failure can be expressed in five words: "I did not have time."
–Franklin Field

271
The higher goal a person pursues, the quicker his ability develops, and the more beneficial he will become to the society. I believe for sure that this is also a truth.
–Maksim Gorky

272
The impossible is often the untried.
–Jim Goodwin

273
The most difficult thing is the decision to act;
the rest is merely tenacity.
–Amelia Earhart

274
The time for action is now.
It's never too late to do something.
–Carl Sandburg

275
The most important question to ask is,
what am I becoming?
–Jim Rohn

276
The most effective way to do it is to do it.
–Amelia Earhart

277
The very essence of leadership is that you have
to have a vision. It's got to be a vision you
articulate clearly and forcefully on every
occasion. You can't blow an uncertain trumpet.
–Reverend Theodore Hesburgh

278
There are no shortcuts to any place worth going.
–Beverly Sills

279
Though no one can go back and make a brand
new start, anyone can start from now and
make a brand new ending.
–Carl Bard

280
Time is a great teacher, but unfortunately
it kills all its pupils.
–Hector Louis Berlioz

281
Time lost is never found again.
–Benjamin Franklin

282
To do great things is difficult; but to command great things is more difficult.
–Friedrich Nietzsche

283
We must believe that we are gifted for something, and that this thing, at whatever cost, must be attained.
–Marie Curie

284
What you get by achieving your goals is not as important as what you become by achieving your goals.
–Zig Ziglar

285
While we are postponing, life speeds by.
–Seneca

286
You can't change the past, but you can ruin the
present by worrying about the future.
–Unknown

287
You cannot do a kindness too soon, for you
never know how soon it will be too late.
–Ralph Waldo Emerson

288
Every day of your working life is part of an
interview for a job you don't even know
you're going for yet.
–Adam Darowski

289
Risk more than others think is safe. Care more than others think is wise. Dream more than others think is practical. Expect more than others think is possible.
–Claude Bissell

290
You never know when a moment and a few sincere words can have an impact on a life.
–Zig Ziglar

291
A hundred years from now it will not matter what my bank account was, the sort of house I lived in, or the kind of car I drove…but the world may be different because I was important in the life of a child.
–Forest Witcraft

292
Establishing goals is all right if you don't let them deprive you of interesting detours.
–Doug Larson

293
Great leaders are almost always great
simplifiers, who can cut through argument,
debate, and doubt to offer a solution
everybody can understand.
–General Colin Powell

294
He does not seem to me to be a free man who
does not sometimes do nothing.
–Cicero

295
He lives long that lives well;
and time misspent is not lived but lost.
–Thomas Fuller

296
I love deadlines. I like the whooshing sound
they make as they fly by.
–Douglas Adams

297

If it weren't for the last minute,
a lot of things wouldn't get done.
–Michael S. Traylor

298

If you want to make good use of your time,
you've got to know what's most important and
then give it all you've got.
–Lee Iacocca

299

If you would hit the mark, you must aim a little
above it; every arrow that flies feels
the attraction of earth.
–Henry Wadsworth Longfellow

300

If you're bored with life —you don't get up every
morning with a burning desire to do things —
you don't have enough goals.
–Lou Holtz

301

It is a most mortifying reflection for a man
to consider what he has done, compared to
what he might have done.
–Samuel Johnson

302

It's how we spend our time here and now, that
really matters. If you are fed up with the way
you have come to interact with time, change it.
–Marcia Wieder

303

Leaders think and talk about the solutions.
Followers think and talk about the problems.
–Brian Tracy

304

Leadership and learning are
indispensable to each other.
–John F. Kennedy

305

Leadership is solving problems. The day soldiers stop bringing you their problems is the day you have stopped leading them. They have either lost confidence that you can help or concluded you do not care. Either case is a failure of leadership.
—General Colin Powell

306

Lost wealth may be replaced by industry, lost knowledge by study, lost health by temperance or medicine, but lost time is gone forever.
—Samuel Smiles

307

Management is about arranging and telling. Leadership is about nurturing and enhancing.
—Tom Peters

308

Only those who will risk going too far can possibly find out how far one can go.
—T.S. Eliot

309
Outstanding leaders go out of their way to boost the self–esteem of their personnel. If people believe in themselves, it's amazing what they can accomplish.
–Sam Walton

310
Perhaps when we find ourselves wanting everything, it is because we are dangerously close to wanting nothing.
–Sylvia Plath

311
Some of the world's greatest feats were accomplished by people not smart enough to know they were impossible.
–Doug Larson

312
Take a rest. A field that has rested yields a beautiful crop.
–Ovid

313
Take the first step in faith.
We don't need to see the whole staircase;
we just need to take the first step.
–Martin Luther King

314
Teach thy tongue to say, "I do not know,"
and thou shalt progress.
–Maimonides

315
The best angle from which to approach any
problem is the try–angle.
–Author Unknown

316
The best executive is the one who has sense
enough to pick good men to do what he wants
done, and self–restraint enough to keep from
meddling with them while they do it.
–Theodore Roosevelt

317
The growth and development of people is the
highest calling of leadership.
–Harvey Firestone

318
The important thing in life is to have a great aim,
and the determination to attain it.
–Johann Wolfgang von Goethe

319
The key to successful leadership today is
influence, not authority.
–Kenneth Blanchard

320
The leader has to be practical and a realist yet
must talk the language of the visionary
and the idealist.
–Eric Hoffer

321

The nation will find it very hard to look up to the leaders who are keeping their ears to the ground.
–Sir Winston Churchill

322

The only person you are destined to become is the person you decide to be.
–Ralph Waldo Emerson

323

The real pleasure of one's life is the devotion to a great objective of one's consideration.
–George Bernard Shaw

324

The rung of a ladder was never meant to rest upon, but only to hold a man's foot long enough to enable him to put the other somewhat higher.
–Thomas Henry Huxley

325
Every no gets me closer to a yes.
–Mark Cuban

326
The time you enjoy wasting is not wasted time.
–Bertrand Russell

327
The world is moving so fast these days that the
man who says it can't be done is generally
interrupted by someone doing it.
–Elbert Hubbard

328
The worst days of those who enjoy what they do
are better than the best days of those who don't.
–Jim Rohn

329

The young do not know enough to be prudent,
and therefore they attempt the impossible –and
achieve it, generation after generation.
–Pearl S. Buck

330

This time, like all times, is a very good one,
if we but know what to do with it.
–Ralph Waldo Emerson

331

Those who make the worse use of their time are
the first to complain of its shortness.
–Jean De La Bruyere

332

Time is a great healer, but a poor beautician.
–Lucille Harper

333
Time is really the only capital that any human
being has, and the only thing he can't
afford to lose.
–Thomas Edison

334
Time is the wisest counselor of all.
–Pericles

335
Time will take your money,
but money won't buy time.
–James Taylor

336
To think too long about doing a thing often
becomes its undoing.
–Eva Young

337
To do two things at once is to do neither.
–Publius Syrus

338
True leadership lies in guiding others to success.
In ensuring that everyone is performing at their
best, doing the work they are pledged to do
and doing it well.
–Bill Owens

339
What is not started today is never
finished tomorrow.
–Johann Wolfgang von Goethe

340
What may be done at any time
will be done at no time.
–Scottish Proverb

341
When everything seems to be going against you,
remember that the airplane takes off against the
wind, not with it.
–Henry Ford

342
When I give a minister an order,
I leave it to him to find the means to carry it out.
–Napoleon Bonaparte

343
Work expands so as to fill the time
available for its completion.
–Cyril Parkinson

344
You gain strength, courage and confidence by
every experience in which you really stop to
look fear in the face. You must do the thing
you think you cannot do.
–Eleanor Roosevelt

345
You may delay, but time will not.
–Benjamin Franklin

346
You must have long–range goals to keep you
from being frustrated by short–range failures.
–Charles C. Noble

347
Your goals are the road maps that guide you and
show you what is possible for your life.
–Les Brown

348
You cannot change your destination overnight,
but you can change your direction overnight.
–Jim Rohn

349
If you obey all the rules, you miss all the fun.
–Katharine Hepburn

350
The best way to succeed
is to double your failure rate.
–Thomas Watson

351
This to shall pass. **–Proverb**

352
After climbing a great hill, one only finds that
there are many more hills to climb.
–Nelson Mandela

353
Winning isn't everything, but wanting to win is.
–Vince Lombardi

354
You can't cross the sea merely by standing
and staring at the water.
–Rabindranath Tagore

355
You don't lead by hitting people over the head–
that's assault, not leadership.
–Dwight Eisenhower

356
You don't lead by pointing and telling people
some place to go. You lead by going to that
place and making a case.
–Ken Kesey

357
A competent leader can get efficient service
from poor troops, while on the contrary an inca-
pable leader can demoralize
the best of troops.
–John Pershing

358
A ruler should be slow to punish
and swift to reward.
–Ovid

359
A straight path never leads anywhere
except to the objective.
–Andre Gide

360
A wise person does at once,
what a fool does at last. Both do the same thing;
only at different times.
–Baltasar Gracián

361
Work like there is someone working 24 hours a
day to take it away from you.
–Mark Cuban

362
The surest way to be late
is to have plenty of time.
–Leo Kennedy

363
The space you occupy and the authority you exercise may be measured with mathematical exactness by the service you render.
–Napoleon Hill

364
If you only knock long enough and loud enough at the gate, you are sure to wake somebody up.
–Henry Longfellow

365
By perseverance the snail reached the ark.
–Charles Spurgeon

BONUS: HOW TO DISCOVER YOUR LIFE'S TRUE PURPOSE

Each of these activities will require you to use your imagination and to reflect deeply. Find a quiet, comfortable spot where you can close your eyes and think in peace. You may want to keep your journal or some paper nearby to record your thoughts.

ACTIVITY ONE: The Rocking Chair Test

It's been said that when we are on our deathbeds we will regret the things we *didn't* do, not the things we did. Imagine that you are 90 years old, fully retired and sitting in a rocking chair out on your porch. Imagine that you are looking back on your 90 years of life. What would be the things that would make you sad, if you never got around to doing them?

Are there places in the world that you would regret never having visited? Are there people in your life you still need to forgive, or to apologize to? Will you regret never having read the Bible, or never having learned to play the piano, or never having learned a foreign language? Who do you still need to thank? In what ways do you want to serve others before you retire?

ACTIVITY TWO: Lottery Winner

OK, if deathbed activities are too much of a downer, how about this one.

Congratulations, you won the (imaginary) lottery! How much? You decide. Pick an amount that is so huge, there is no way you'd ever have to work again. Pick an amount so big that you'd have money to spend at will. Ten million dollars? A hundred million? A billion? You pick.

Now truly imagine you won that much money. You can do anything you want to do! So what would you do? Sure, sure you'd buy sports cars and planes and vacation homes— what the heck, buy some islands. OK, you got all the toys out of the way, and still have so many years of your life to fill. What would you do? How would you spend your time?

Would you write a book? If so, on what topic? Would you still want to start a business even though you didn't need the money? Is there a special charity you'd like to support, or maybe even *start*. Who would you want to help with your money? Family and friends are probably on your list, but who else comes to mind? Homeless veterans? Orphans? Abandoned pets?

ACTIVITY THREE: What Gives You Energy?

Isn't it funny how time can move so slowly when we're in a long boring meeting at work, or waiting in the dentist's chair?

And yet other times you've probably experienced states of "flow" where the hours just fly by and you can't believe what time it is.

Try to remember the times and experiences that have flown by and given you energy—times when your work or play may have been challenging, but totally engaging. Do you get energy when you are alone, or with other people? Are your flow states typically when you are working with your hands, or working more cerebrally? Do you get lost (in a good way) figuring out the details of projects, or thinking of big picture vision? Are you a creator—do you like to create things whether they are books, businesses, or artwork?

Now it's time to put it all together. Take the clues that come from imaging regrets, passions, flow-states and the types of people you like to serve. Put it all together to specifically answer:

- What are the things you most like doing?
- Who do you want to serve?
- How might you benefit them?

There is no "right" way to write your purpose statement, but you might find inspiration from some of these specific examples:

- "My purpose is to teach entrepreneurship to those in less developed countries so they, and future generations, can live a more prosperous life."
- "My purpose is to model positive values and healthy living for my children, so they might adopt healthy and happy lifestyles as adults."

- "My purpose is to create unique smartphone games for people who want to experience more joy in their life."
- "My purpose is to be a role-model of servant leadership so working professionals can maximize their engagement and productivity at work."

Working on your personal purpose statement—or mission statement—can bring you both greater inner peace, and more daily motivation knowing you are serving your ultimate purpose.

And don't forget, your purpose can change. As you live, you grow. You will have new experiences, new relationships, new learnings that will impact. Don't be afraid to grow your purpose along the way.